Bygone GOVAN

by

George Rountree

This photograph of St Mary's Govan Cross football team was taken *c.*1914, probably at the sports ground on the riverside at the foot of Rathlin Street. The land was later taken over by either Fairfield's or Harland & Wolff. My father, George Rountree, is right of centre in the middle row, and David Brooks is on the left in the back row.

© George Rountree 2003
First published in the United Kingdom, 2003
reprinted 2007,
by Stenlake Publishing limited
Tel: 01290 551122
www.stenlake.co.uk

Printed in the United Kingdom
by St Edmundsbury Press,
Bury St Edmunds, IP33 3TU

ISBN 9781840332650

The publishers regret that they cannot supply copies of any pictures featured in this book.

ACKNOWLEDGEMENTS
I would like to thank the following people and organisations for providing pictures and information. Members of the Govan Reminiscence Group (GRG) who allowed me to use a number of photographs and postcards from their archives, and John Simpson who checked the captions and from whose collection of slides now in the care of GRG I selected several. Richard Stenlake provided a significant number of postcards and other pictures, and Graham McLachlan contributed information on naval matters and dock and shipyard railways. Thanks to Alan Godfrey of Gateshead for old maps, the late Chris Fletcher for the drawings on pages 4 and 47, and The Herald & Evening Times (Newsquest) Ltd. for permission to use the picture on page 45. Some of the captions include abridged extracts from my book *A Govan Childhood – the 1930s* (now out of print but available in some Glasgow libraries). Much of the rest of the writing, severely condensed, comes from the unpublished second volume, *In Peace and War*.
   The publishers would like to thank Robert Grieves for providing the pictures on pages 15 and 20.

FURTHER READING
The books listed below were used by the author during his research. None of them are available from Stenlake Publishing. Those interested in finding out more are advised to contact their local bookshop or reference library.

Brotchie, T. C. F., *The History Of Govan*, 1938
Donnelly, Pat, *Govan on the Clyde*, 1994
Greenwood, Cedric, *Glasgow Trammerung (Twilight of the Glasgow Tram)*
Little, Stewart, *Glasgow Buses*, 1990
Riddle, John F., *Clyde Navigation*, 1979
Riddle, John F., *The Clyde*, 1988
Robertson J. & Pateman R., *Govan Road*, 1987
Rountree, George, *A Govan Childhood – the 1930s*, 1993
Simpson, John, *A History of Govan*, 1988
Simpson, John, *Govan Past & Present*, 1988
Smith, W. A. C. & Anderson, Paul, *An Illustrated History of Glasgow's Railways*, 1993
Smith, W. A. C. & Anderson, Paul, *Rails Around Glasgow*
Spalding, Bill, *Old Govan*, 1994
Stewart, Ian, *The Glasgow Tramcar*, 1983
Stewart, Ian, *Glasgow By Tram*, 1977
Stewart, Ian, *More Glasgow By Tram*, 1978
Stewart, Ian, *Round Glasgow By Tram*, 1979
Williams, Riches & Higgs, *The Buildings of Scotland, Glasgow*, 1990

Situated on the west corner of Govan Road and Broomloan Road, the Govan branch of the Savings Bank of Glasgow was known as the 'potted heid bank'. I remember being with my mother in the 1930s when she visited the bank and asking why it had that name, because in my mind potted head (brawn) was associated with the butcher's. She pointed to the granite facing panels and said 'Don't you think that looks like potted head?'. That name has, like the granite, endured with me, although someone else told me they thought the bank got its name because of the inverted pudding-bowl shaped cap on top of the tower above the entrance, similar to the glass containers in which the potted head was sold at butchers. The building was probably faced with Peterhead granite, which might have been a factor in the name too!

INTRODUCTION

As both Bill Spalding's *Old Govan* and Pat Donnelly's *Govan on the Clyde* include a brief history of the area, I've not gone over familiar ground in this introduction, but have instead included some personal reminiscences of my childhood in Govan, where I lived up to the age of fourteen.

Like most tenement blocks in the west of Scotland, the ground plan of the one my family lived in at 12 Skipness Drive between 1937 and 1945 was an enclosed oblong containing individual back courts separated by spiked railings. The buildings or 'dykes' in the centre were composed of wash-houses and middens (refuse stores), one of each for each close, with four on either side of the block's long axis standing back to back, and pairs of individual detached buildings for the four closes in each end of the block. At eight feet in height with slightly sloping concrete roofs, the dykes were a magnet for adventurous children. The layout of the buildings meant that there were gaps of different widths between them which provided challenging jumps of varying degrees of difficulty. Access to their roofs was gained by climbing up a drainpipe or onto one of the railings at the point where it abutted the dyke wall; from there standing on top of the spikes brought the roof to chest height and it was easy to scramble up. When the gaps between our own dykes had been mastered (helped by much daring and goading of each other), we began to trek round neighbouring blocks looking for other challenges to further test our nerve. As time passed we became more experienced, occasionally returning to try and conquer those that had defeated us last time round. Looking back the dangers were appalling, largely because of what we might have landed on had we fallen off. In those days railings were almost universally spiked to deter climbers – all were dangerous, but some were lethal, with those separating back courts among the worst, having slim, sharp spikes. Concerns of parents were understandable, knowing their offspring were larking about and forgetting the danger, and their dilemma was great in not wishing to call their children off and give them a showing-up in front of their pals. At the age of seven I was warned off a few times in private, but the obvious way to avoid being seen was to go to one of the neighbouring blocks and climb there, hoping that no-one knew your parents and would tell on you. Stories circulated of impalements, and although there were no fatalities I remember one boy of brief acquaintance showing off two piercing scars in a thigh!

The 1936 photograph on this page is one of only two back court scenes in this book (the other one is the chums photograph on page 32). Visible is part of the dyke behind 13 Hutton Drive (where my maternal grandparents lived), with the rear of the Drive Road tenement in the background. Behind me in the picture, of all things, is the midden! The wash-house with its 'lum' just visible is on the left, while on the right is part of the dividing wall between the two streets of tenements, occupying the space between the group of wash-house/midden buildings visible here and the adjacent group. This photograph would have been taken not long after the slate barrier had been removed from midden entrances and bins installed for the rubbish. Prior to that time, rubbish, mainly ashes from domestic fires, was simply thrown in to mount up until the cleansing department 'scaffies' (a name probably derived from scavengers) called to shovel it into large baskets and humph it out through the close to the rubbish truck waiting in the street. Each midden and wash-house had a curved tile ventilator on its cast concrete roof.

Aside from the midden, the other building to be located in the back court was the wash-house. Access to this, where most tenants did their weekly wash, was allocated in 'turns', mornings or afternoons, among the tenants of the twelve houses in the close. It was a room about twelve feet by ten with walls of rough brick and a concrete floor and roof, in a corner of which stood a large copper boiler with a loose lid. This was set within a squat, round brick housing standing to waist height. Under the boiler, which was filled from a tap, there was a fireplace with a raised nest and a flue which rose up in the corner to a chimney-head on the roof. Next to the door, against the outer wall and below the window, there were two large, white glazed pottery tubs, each with a cold water tap. In the case of those women whose turn was in the morning, the fire had to be set at an early hour and attended for stoking so that the water would be boiling in good time – no later than 9 o'clock. If her husband was up for work early enough or willing to rise earlier, he carried the paper, sticks and coal down, lighting the fire and filling the boiler for his wife. She then took over, and when the water was boiling about half of it was transferred to a tub and cooled to hand temperature to wash coloured clothes. The boiling water had to be scooped from the boiler and carried to one of tubs using a large tin ladle with a wooden handle which held about half a gallon, and scalding accidents were an occupational hazard. White clothes were put into the boiler itself with soap powder and perhaps some Dolly Blue whitener.

After a period of boiling, the whites were transferred to one of the tubs using a heavy-duty brush pole so that the hot, dripping clothes could be manipulated from a safe distance. The actual washing was done using a washboard, a flat wooden frame with legs which stood about two feet high by eighteen inches wide. There was a ledge at the top to hold the washing soap and scrubbing brush; below this was a sheet of ribbed glass or textured steel or aluminium for rubbing the clothes on. The feet of the board rested in the tub, with the upper part leaning against its edge, giving a comfortable angle for scrubbing the soapy clothes, which were alternately dipped and scrubbed. Having been washed, the first batch of clothes was then put through the wringer and into the other tub to be rinsed, before being put through the wringer again and hung out to dry. There was a raised wooden batten in the space between the tubs on which the wringer was mounted. A predecessor of the spin dryer and made by Acme, a Bridgeton company, this squeezed most of the water from the washed clothes and each household had one. Wringers had two spring-loaded rollers mounted horizontally and geared together, and were operated by a handle similar to the starting handle of contemporary motor vehicles. Pressure on the wringer rollers could be adjusted by turning a round metal knob on top of the wringer body. A big disadvantage of the wringer was that it was severe on clothes, and buttons in particular tended to get broken. Fingers too needed careful watching, particularly if two people were involved. The drawing of a wash-house shown here is accurate in all but one respect: what has been drawn as a low bench was in fact a table.

tile vent

flue

duckboard

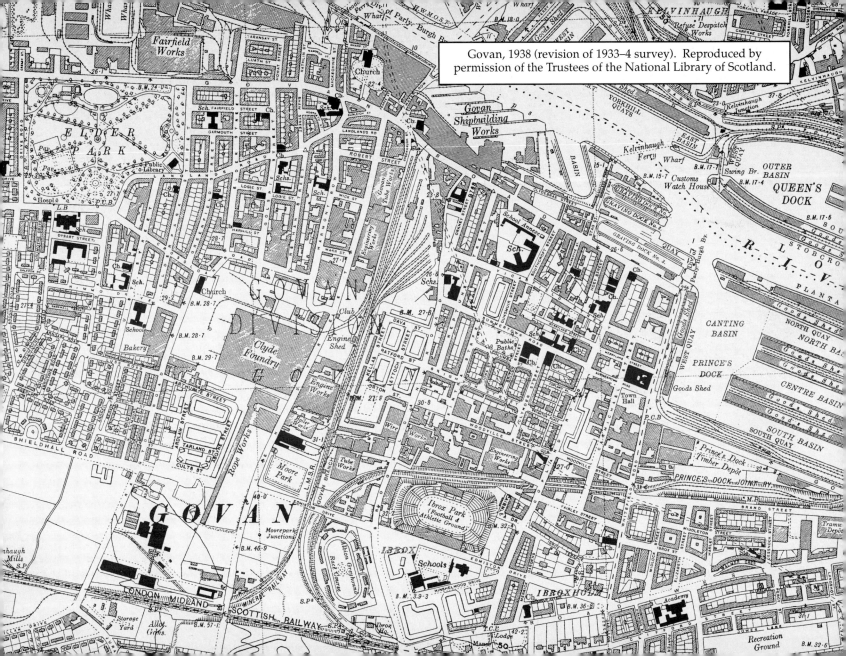

Admiral Street, 1958. Glasgow Corporation Transport Department's Standard car No. 334 is at the terminus of the No. 12 service, with an inspector, probably the Paisley Road Toll timekeeper, standing on the step in conference with the driver. At peak periods the service continued to Linthouse for shipyard workers by turning left into Paisley Road West, then travelling along Lorne Street to join Govan Road at Brand Street. Behind the tramcar is the Imperial Cinema, with one of the iron ore grab-bucket cranes of General Terminus Quay beyond it. Ships loaded with ore for the Clyde ironworks at Carmyle and Ravenscraig steelworks at Motherwell docked here, where these massive cranes grabbed the ore out of the holds and fed it onto elevated conveyor belts which took it over the road. The ore was then fed into vast silos, before being weighed and dropped into 24-ton capacity hopper railway waggons. The waggons were shunted out to the marshalling yard which lay between Seaward Street and Shields Road, then made up into trains of 28 vehicles with a brake van at each end, ready to be hauled away by pairs of class 20 (type 1) diesel locomotives.

Paisley Road Toll, Glasgow.

Today Paisley Road Toll (seen here *c*.1920) marks the eastern extremity of the Plantation district, but this area lay within Govan Burgh boundary until 1912. Ogg Brothers' department store faced east along Paisley Road, and the statue of an angel on its roof (not visible in this picture, but still in place today) meant that it came to be known as the Angel Building. The Ogg family also owned the larger Copeland & Lye store in Sauchiehall Street. Behind Ogg Bros. and running between Paisley Road West (with tramcar) and Govan Road (right) was the gently curving Rutland Crescent, with an offshoot into the rear of the Ogg building called Lauriston Lane, used by the store for goods access. The building had a basement with amusements which included dodgem cars. Beyond the crescent there was Rutland Lane and Mair Street; it is probably the latter which can be seen along Govan Road. To the left and out of frame lies the Kinning Park district. Admiral Street branched off at this point, and the Imperial Cinema was built around this time to the photographer's right facing up the street. The eight-sided building in front of Ogg's provided shelter for people awaiting public transport. In the early years of the twentieth century, adjacent to the cinema, there was a post at the inside edge of the pavement which was reputed to have once supported the toll barrier.

Govan Road, Plantation, 1958, with the junction of Eaglesham Street on the left. Car 1367, a mark II Coronation type on the No. 4 service, is bound for Hillington Road. The bus in the background is a Leyland PD2, while to its right is the domed building of the original Clyde Tunnel. The tunnel had twin shafts, and access was by stairs for pedestrians and a hydraulic lift for vehicles, both of which were located within the domes (there was one on each side of the river). My grandfather once took me for a walk through the tunnel, and as we were going down the stairs we became aware of a carter having difficulty with his horse in the open vehicle lift shaft. The 'cuddy' was alarmed by the motion of the lift, but the carter managed to calm it by gripping the reigns firmly close to its mouth with one hand and holding the other over its nose. Just to the right of the nearest advertisement hoarding and behind the larger building was office of the Dock Labour Board, which regulated the employment of the dockers. In the background are the jibs of dockside cranes and masts and funnels of ships moored at Mavisbank and Plantation Quays. The Finnieston crane is on the right.

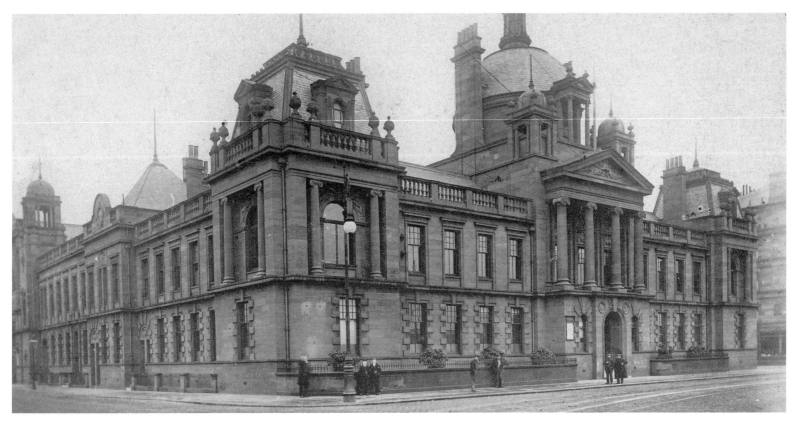

Govan's first municipal chambers were located at Hillock House which stood opposite Govan railway goods station on ground where the fabrication shed of Harland & Wolff's shipyard was later built. Hillock House was named after the nearby Doomster Hill, an ancient barrow or burial mound which probably dated from pre-Roman times. It gradually disappeared as industrial development progressed in the area. New council chambers were built in Orkney Street in 1867, and these were in use until 1901 when rapid expansion of the burgh meant that larger premise were required. After 1901 the buildings in Orkney Street were used by the burgh, corporation, and later Glasgow District Council as a police office and fire station. This ornate new building at 401 Govan Road was constructed between 1897 and 1901, and its appearance today continues to reflects the prosperity of the burgh at that time. At the same time the council was building swimming baths further along Summertown Road, which were also opened in 1901. The outlook from and appearance of the new building was further enhanced by having the open prospect of the canting basin of Cessnock (Prince's) Dock (1897) opposite. People in west Govan, however, complained the hall was too remote for them so another one was built (1923–6) by Glasgow Corporation at the corner of Langlands Road and Arklet Road, Drumoyne. It was called South Govan Town Hall, and when it opened the prefix 'Old' was applied to the name of the main hall at Summertown Road.

Govan Road photographed in 1958 with Prince's Dock to the right. Vicarfield Street is next on the left and beyond that is Elphinstone Street. The tram is Coronation No. 1355, operating on service 4 to the intermediate terminus at Shieldhall. In the distance a bus is rounding what was then the sharp curve at the north-west corner of the dock, while the nearer vehicle, partly obscured by the lorry, is on the No. 4 service between Drumoyne and Balornock. The canting basin was located at the western end of Prince's Dock and on its quay, but unfortunately out of frame in this picture, was a static 130-ton steam heavy-lift crane. This was mainly used for loading steam locomotives built for foreign railways at Springburn onto ships, as well as by shipyards with no suitable lifting capacity of their own to install engines and boilers. 'Canting' was the term used to describe the manoeuvring of a ship with tugs in a confined space. At the turn of the twentieth century bunkering (taking on coal to fire ships' boilers) was a major operation which accounted for a high proportion of dockside work. From 1903 there was a coal loading facility at the head of the canting basin.

At 880 feet, Graving Dock No. 3 was the most modern and longest of the three graving docks which stood side by side on this site. When it was opened in 1898 it could accommodate the largest vessel then afloat, while the steel gates near its centre could be closed to allow work to be carried out independently on two smaller vessels. Over time sludge accumulated on the bottom so a clean-up had to be occasionally undertaken, something that seems to have just been completed here. The sediment was shovelled into the large buckets seen here, which were then lifted out by the dockside travelling crane. Ships would have to be carefully centred in the dry dock so that their keels rested on the line of heavy timbers in the centre, while the other timbers towards the sides may have been to support the bilge keels if a ship had them. For additional stability the timbers laid out along the dockside were lowered by crane and butted on the most convenient step, with the other end braced against the ship's side. Note the eight step accesses in and out of the basin, two on either side in each section, which led through the walls of the graving dock to surface among the timbers and mooring posts. The two streets branching off from the tenements of Govan Road are Hoey Street and Burndyke Street, while at the far end of the dock, behind the wall, is Stag Street with an access road off it to dock level.

This is Harland & Wolff's (normally referred to simply as Harland's) battery-powered locomotive, which trundled with short trains of loaded waggons across Govan Road from the middle set of the three goods yard gates at Govan Cross goods station into the fabrication shed through large sliding double doors (just out of sight in the picture opposite). According to the 1913 Ordnance Survey map, the point where the track entered the shed is precisely where Hillock House (see page 9) and Hillock Place were situated. While it wasn't as extensive as Fairfield's, Harland's internal railway system covered all their premises, with an extension across Water Row into the platers shed to the west. The practice was loads in, empties out as soon as possible to avoid the demurrage charge levied by the companies which owned the waggons that the locomotive pulled. Before this charge was introduced customers tended to leave loads stored on the waggons until they needed them, which meant that expensive rolling stock could be tied up for lengthy periods. My dad worked in the Govan Shafting & Engineering Co. in Helen Street which had a siding adjacent to the goods yard for deliveries of materials. He said the demurrage charges were so hefty they were obliged to unload waggons and return them as quickly as possible. The wires seemingly above the cab in this picture are over the adjacent line and carried the current supply for Fairfield's locomotive. Govan Cross goods station was opened for passengers and goods in 1868, but because of competition from trams the passenger service was discontinued in 1921, although the platforms were still visible into the 1950s.

Looking east from Govan Cross in 1958. On the extreme left is part of St Mary's Free Church, with a tenement beyond it and then Harland's platers shed. The Plaza Cinema is in the middle ground with a British Railways sign behind the railings bordering Govan Cross goods station. The tram is Coronation No. 1346 on the No. 4 service bound for Hillington Road. In the foreground are the tracks used by the Fairfield goods train to reach the goods yard. A. & J. Morrice's newsagent's and stationer's shop on the right at the corner of Greenhaugh Street is memorable because although I never owned one, it was here that I saw my first Hornby train set. Greenhaugh Street and Robert Street were the termini for seven bus services: the 4A to Croftfoot; the 17 to Penilee via Hillington; the 23 to the Broomielaw via Moss Road, Crookston Road and Barrhead Road; the 25 to Hillington Estate via Queensland Drive; the 26 to Priesthill; the 36 to Hillington Estate via Renfrew Road; and the 49 to Nitshill via Hurlet.

St Mary's Free Church at Govan Cross was built in the Gothic style in 1873, and is now called Govan New Church. My father's side of the family were members of this church from the early 1890s. In 1929 the Free Church rejoined the Church of Scotland (having broken away from it in the Disruption of 1843) causing a split in the congregation. Although the majority were in favour of rejoining, a number of members (including my father's family) were not and set up a place of worship opposite in Govan Cross Mansions. After a time they moved to better accommodation in Burndyke Street,

and by the 1930s had managed to raise enough funds to have a church of their own built on a site in Moss Road, opposite the junction with Langlands Road. Built in 1934/35, it was called Shieldhall and Drumoyne Church and survived until the mid-1960s when Moss Road was widened to accommodate the Clyde Tunnel dual carriageway. Fortunately there was enough land at the rear of the plot at Carleith Quadrant for a replacement church to be built. This was set back from the line of first one by about 30 feet. In addition to demolishing the church, all the top-quality four-in-a-block corporation houses along the west side of Moss Road, built in the mid-1920s, were demolished to make way for the new road. Church records can be an important source of information for the family history researcher. In the 1980s I asked to consult them at St Mary's but was told there were none; they had been lost in a fire at a church officer's house. Some time later I met a fellow researcher who was able to quote from them. She said she was put off with the same story of the fire, but kept asking and her persistence paid off when she found that the fire had occurred in the 1890s and records were available from after this time. The trees just visible at the extreme right-hand edge of this picture date it to the 1890s or even earlier. Note also Doctor Aitken's fountain on the left, the railing round the entrance to the underground gents' toilet, and the sign pointing to the Water Row ferry.

OLD WATER ROW & HORSE FERRY.

Water Row seen from Yorkhill *c.*1900. In the dock is one of the original steam- and chain-operated vehicular ferries of the type known as horse ferries; there is a place on the Thames still bearing that name. From the earliest days of industrial development, the banks of the river were continuous rights of way for pedestrians, and shipyards and other businesses which set up there had to maintain public access. Boardwalks were built over the slipways at shipyards and were only removed for launches. In this picture the path can be seen at a higher level on the left of the ferry from where it passes round the head of the ferry slip. It continues in front of the whitewashed buildings to exit at the right between the fencing. Of the four old buildings, the two farthest from the river were demolished in 1911, but the others survived until Harland's shipyard was established *c.*1917. The narrow Water Row ran between the two fairly new tenements seen on the left. Harland's rail connection extended from their premises (left), crossing Water Row in front of the tenements and entering the platers' shed on the right, which was built to the same design and using the same materials as the shed in Govan Road. The jumble of buildings in the right background include the Pearce Institute, various tenements and a Baptist Church.

This view looking west from the Cross *c.*1950 was taken from the top deck rear vestibule of a Standard tram travelling east. The centre window could be lowered to any height, which was convenient in warm weather and for photography, although the rope for pulling over the Fischer bow current collector on the roof, which looped down here, had to be avoided. The parallel lines in the cobbles about a foot outside the trackbed marked the boundary between the transport and road maintenance departments' responsibilities. On the corner of Water Row (right) is a branch of the British Linen Bank, with the main post office beyond it on Govan Road. The YMCA tenement known as Govan Cross Mansions (out of sight in this view) also stood in Water Row. It is about half past three in the afternoon and the sun is streaming along Helen Street and over the main road. Beyond the junction of Helen Street is the 'black man' statue and the Cardell Hall with its pokey-hat roof above the stairs. The statue, of Sir William Pearce, is so-called because it was cast in bronze which suffered from atmospheric contamination and turned black. The Pearce Institute with its projecting clock is opposite, and the Coronation 'Cunarder' tram is passing Pearce Street. The Lyceum Cinema is in the distance.

The eastern section of this block, bordered by Helen Street (right), Langlands Road (left), Burleigh (formerly Morrison) Street and Harmony Row was occupied by the central premises of Kinning Park Co-operative Society at basement, ground and first floor level. This section of Langlands Road had previously been called James Place. The store nearest the camera was the furnishing department, with drapery and mantles adjoining it (where the shopfitting work is taking place) and continuing round the next corner and into Burleigh Street. Other stores located in the building were footware, soft furnishings, hardware, a dairy, butchers, and a grocery. In 1950 the Kinning Park Co-op amalgamated with the Pollokshaws Co-op and the group became the Glasgow South Co-operative Society.

St Anthony's infant/primary school was in Harmony Row, tucked away on a cramped site at the rear of St Anthony's Church (built 1877). Demolition of nearby tenements has since opened up the prospect, and today it is difficult to appreciate just how enclosed the former school building was. The postage-stamp sized playground was completely surrounded by buildings. My mother and her sister Molly, who lived at 16 Harmony Row, attended the school until 1912, and my mother used to tell of how the kitchen window looked into the classrooms. I too

attended the infants' school for a year from the family home in Howat Street, until we moved to Linthouse in 1937. My mother, Agnes Chambers, is fifth from the left in the middle row of this class photograph, taken at St Anthony's *c*.1910. Her sister Molly is on the left of the front row. My recollections of St Anthony's are of thick, dark paper and crayons used for drawing, the sand tray, slates, slate pencils and a duster for wiping the slates clean. The sand tray was used to practice writing letters of the alphabet in with a finger.

The Lyceum Cinema at 918 Govan Road (the corner of McKechnie Street) opened as a theatre in 1899. Its debut show was a performance by an opera company, but as films became increasingly popular it began to put on mixed programmes of music hall acts, comedy and short silent films. In 1923 the theatre closed to be converted to a cinema, but a fire in 1935 destroyed much of it and in 1937 it was rebuilt with greater capacity in art deco style. The Lyceum is the only one of Govan's five cinema buildings to have survived (it has been a bingo hall since 1981). The others were the Elder in Rathlin Street; the Plaza at the Cross (east of the railway goods station); and the Vogue (built 1937) at the junction of Crossloan Road and Langlands Road. The fifth one, whose name I don't know, was in Helen Street at Greenhaugh Street. (Two other local cinemas, the Imperial at Paisley Road Toll and the Capitol in Lorn Street, were outwith Govan's boundaries.) In the early days of cinema, a number of halls around Govan were temporarily used to show films, one of which was at the corner of White (Golspie) Street and Langlands Road.

Govan Road looking west from Howat Street (out of shot to the right) in 1958, with the junction of Golspie Street on the left. In the tenement between Howat Street and Elder Street, which the bus is seen approaching, there was another suite of Kinning Park Co-op shops (by this time it was the Glasgow South Co-op), identifiable by the long, light-coloured headboard. The address of the shops was 1000–1004 Govan Road. George Munley's radio and gramophone shop, Govan Music House, is behind the pole with the tall white band on the right. Aside from primitive crystal sets which needed no power supply, most wireless sets in the early 1930s were powered by lead/acid accumulators rather larger than present day motorcycle batteries. They were heavy, made of thick glass, had a metal carrying bracket, and had to be returned to premises like Munley's or to a garage with electrical charging facilities for recharging, the life between charges lasting, according to use, about a month. To the right of the bus is the entrance to Fairfield's shipyard, from which a drift of steam is emanating. This could only have come from their last steam engine, which was sent for scrap in 1960.

Langlands Road looking east from Greenfield Street *c*.1930. Sun blinds were essential to protect perishable goods on display in shops on the sunny side of the street, and here windows are well covered but in a rather untidy way. In the background at the corner of White Street (which became Golspie Street in 1930) is the Govan Evangelical Union (later Congregational) Church of 1882. Sometime after 1913 tracks were laid so that trams could travel up Golspie Street from the junction seen in the picture on the previous page. They turned into Langlands Road where the span wires are visible here, then travelled south along Elder Street, continuing via Crossloan Road and Craigton Road to the No. 7 terminus at Bellahouston.

Golspie Street photographed *c.*1970 with the Salvation Army building of 1903 in the foreground. Notarianni's Cafe was located in the tenement opposite here. Their ice cream was reputed to be the best in Govan, and during the 1930s the family had a horse-drawn ice cream cart with a very pleasing livery which matched that of the cafe – creamy yellow with narrow vertical black stripes running down from a horizontal line at waist level. On one occasion in Linthouse in 1937 I was among a throng of young customers in Skipness Drive buying a 'pokey hat'. The woman serving caught my eye and asked me to buy a paper from nearby Dick's newsagents in Kennedar Drive. When I returned with it and asked for a cone, she heaped it up with so much extra ice cream that half of it melted before I could eat it! Later the Notoriannis acquired a motor van with the same livery as the cart. The tenement in the left background, seen on the right on page 19, stands in Govan Road between Elder Street and Howat Street.

Langlands Road at Nethan Street *c.*1950. The Fairfield Drapery Store is having a closing down sale, and it looks as if part of the premises on the right are already being reconstructed for another business. The sign on the corner reads 'Milliners' (a stockist of women's hats). This photograph was taken looking north from Nethan Street (formerly Hamilton Street) with Shaw Street in the background. Of the two shops seen in Shaw Street, J. Holmes's seems to have been – before the term came into use – a DIY store with rolls of wallpaper on display, and Jean Sandeman's a dairy. Note the surviving Victorian ornamental lamp-post complete with (modern) wire rubbish basket attached.

The Fairfield shipyard, probably photographed in the 1920s. Note the connecting corridor for office personnel above the gate between the two office buildings. This gate, on rollers, was opened two or three times a day to allow goods trains to enter and leave the premises using the tram tracks between the yard and Govan Cross goods station. Railway vehicle wheels had deeper flanges than those on the tramcars, so the waggon wheels ran with the flanges in the rail grooves. The rail junction is visible here curving off to the right in line with the overhead electric power supply. In the early days of the yard steam locomotives were used for this work, and over the decades it had four steam locos, all built by Andrew Barclay of Kilmarnock, with a maximum of two in use at any one time. The last one was built in 1929 and survived until it was sold for scrap in 1960. In later years there were two steeplecab electric locomotives, the first of which may have been built by Fairfield themselves. This was sold to Glasgow Corporation Transport Department in 1939 for use at Pinkston power station (Port Dundas), which generated the power for the tramway system. The second locomotive was built by English Electric in 1940 and worked until rail traffic ceased in 1966. It was sold to the Scottish Railway Preservation Society at Falkirk in 1967. On the corner of Elder Street (right) is the Fairfield Restaurant, a private venture situated as close as it was possible to get to the yard's main gate.

An early view of Fairfield's main office building in Govan Road. As no tram power cables are visible, it must still have been the era of horse-drawn trams (the tram system was electrified between 1898 and 1902). On the right is the corner of Thomson Street (which became Elderpark Street in 1912), while on the left, where the office building was extended in 1940, is the start of a boundary wall which continued as far as the tenements at Abukir Street in Linthouse. Near its western extremity there was a large angled gate with another east-facing rail access. In addition to the timekeeper's office for employees at the main gate, there was a row of narrow doors in the wall to the immediate left of here which provided a quick exit for the large number of workers who didn't carry a 'piece' so that they could dash home at dinner time. In the early 1900s the yard employed up to 7,000 people. During the 1930s Neil McCulloch's cycle shop was one of those on the right; another was T. Austin's funeral undertaker's premises. My father was hurrying home from an Independent Labour Party (ILP) meeting in Govan during the air-raid of 13 March 1941 when a landmine crashed through the roof of the boiler shop behind these offices. When it exploded it caused the plate glass window of the undertaker's to shatter and crash out on top of him. Fortunately he was unhurt.

Key:

1. Light machine shop
2. Boiler erecting shop
3. Fitting and boiler shop
4. Heavy machine shop
5. Fitting and gearing shops
6. Erecting shops
7. Boiler shop
8. Flanging shop
9. Funnel shop
10. Riggers loft
11. Power station
12. Foundry
13. Apprentice's school
14. Brass finishing shop
15. Turbine blading shop
16. Coppersmiths shop
17. Pipe shop
18. Pipe shop
19. Pattern shop
20. Pattern stores
21. Smithy
22. Cabinet and joiners shops
23. Platers sheds
24. Platers sheds under construction
25. Mould loft
26. Offices

An aerial view of Fairfield's yard dating from 1960. The reduction of shipping activity on the river since the war is apparent, with only two commercial vessels discharging grain at Meadowside Quay into the storage buildings of Meadowside Granary (demolished in 2003). The centre section was first to be built in 1914, second was the eastern extension (begun in 1935 and completed in 1938), and here the third part is under construction in 1960. All were brick-built and of massive bulk. There is still a reasonable amount of activity in Fairfield's basin with three new ships, two of which are naval – a frigate and possibly a corvette – in the fitting-out basin. The frigate must be the Salisbury Class HMS *Lincoln* (F99), which was completed by the yard in 1960. At lower right is Govan Road and Elder Park, but the *K13* monument which stands about 30 feet inside the park's main entrance is not discernible in the picture. *K13* was a submarine built by Fairfield's which, while on trials in the Gareloch in 1917, submerged with an open hatch and was lost along with many lives. The two rectangles of tenements at the right-hand edge of the picture are bounded by Govan Road, Howat Street, Elder Street and Taransay Street, with Luath Street separating the two blocks.

Largest Crane in the World. Height 170 ft. Length of Jib 238 ft. Lifting Capacity 250 tons.
Fairfield Shipbuilding Yard, Govan.

68301.J.V.

As the postcard caption states, this hammerhead crane, built in 1910 at Fairfield's yard, was the largest in the world. This view probably dates from soon after its completion, as the massive set of sheerlegs that the crane would have made redundant are still in situ.

This early view of Elder Park, taken perhaps in 1885, the year it opened, and before the trees and bushes grew to obscure the scene, shows the main entrance off Govan Road (right) and the layout of the principal paths on the north side. On the left the flagpole is seen in a position farther north than it was to be in later years, while in the centre are the buildings of the former Fairfield farm. These were subsequently used as the residence of the park superintendent and by the Corporation Parks Department for storing equipment. Hothouses for plant propagation were built later just beyond the pond, while another building to appear subsequently was made of red brick and stood close to the main road; this was used to store the large competition model yachts. Beyond the park there was another farm, Holmfauldhead farm, which stood roughly where George (Skipness) Drive met Holmfauldhead Drive. When this picture was taken none of the Linthouse tenements on the south side of Govan Road and in Drive Road had been put up. The clock tower of what was then Merryflatts Poorhouse is visible in the distance here.

In 1852 John Elder (b. 1824) became a co-partner in the Govan shipbuilding firm of Randolph, Elliot & Co. The main partners retired in 1868 and John Elder died in 1869, but he was held in such high esteem that the directors of the continuing company renamed it John Elder & Co. It retained this name until 1885 when it became the Fairfield Shipbuilding & Engineering Co. Ltd. John Elder was responsible for devising improvements in the performance of steam engines in ships which made them significantly more economical to operate. This statue of him, life-size and in bronze, was unveiled in 1888. The people of Govan enjoyed the benefactions of John Elder mainly through his wife, Isabella, who funded many improvements in the burgh from the fortune she inherited from her husband. The name Elder is still

Elder Statue, Elder Park, Govan.   RELIABLE [WR] SERIES.

prominent today, adorning local hospitals, the park and the library. Mrs Elder also contributed to the parish church, a training home for nurses, and set up foundations at Glasgow University. She was honoured with her own statue, unveiled in the park in 1906. Opened in 1885, Elder Park had tall cast iron gates and boundary railings, and opening and closing times were strictly observed – dawn to dusk in winter and 7 a.m. to 10 p.m. in summer. The times were displayed on large notice boards at most entrances, along with a long list of regulations for the younger ones to ignore at their peril. In the 1930s eagle-eyed park keepers equipped with whistles were always on duty when the park was open, walking around in smart dark green uniforms, which included a peaked cap. The continuous broad boundary strip of trees and bushes, and other patches within the park, were no-go areas, as were some carefully manicured patches of grass which had many cast-iron KEEP OFF THE GRASS signs laid out at ground level. Facilities included two each of putting greens, tennis courts and bowling greens, and an excellent children's play area in the north-west corner of the park, much of which was lost when the traffic roundabout was built in Govan Road at Drive Road. When the swing park closed it was replaced with a poor imitation near the tennis courts, taking up space in one of the areas used for ball games.

A 1928 view of the bandstand in Elder Park, with Fairfield's sheds and their 250 ton hammerhead crane in the background. Of the two boys on the right the younger one has a 'parish' haircut, short all over except for the longer tuft at the front. Behind the man with the dog there was a tree-lined avenue leading to the main gate near Elderpark Street. Some were the poplars seen here, but there were others which I think were sycamores, one of which lay at a very steep angle. During a severe storm in the late 1930s there was a brilliant flash of lightning and a deafening and simultaneous peal of thunder. The heavy rain accompanying the fireworks had gathered to run down the underside of the trunk of the leaning tree, providing a path for a lightning strike, and a large section of its bark was burned off. A favourite band which gave regular concerts in Elder Park during the summer months was the Govan Salvation Army Citadel, although other bands from around the city and further afield also visited. The platform-edge apron of the bandstand was very ornate, with mouldings illustrating shipbuilding, music and art. At the beginning of the Second World War the bandstand was demolished by having a rope tied round one of its legs and attached to the back of a lorry. When the lorry was driven forward the whole structure collapsed and the pieces were gathered up and sent off as a contribution to the war effort. A barrage balloon was installed in 1940 in the area to the left of here.

The pond, Elder Park, c.1910. Although large model yachts of the sort belonging to adults (being too expensive for boys!) are being sailed on the pond, the yacht store was not built until later. Colder winters in the 1930s and 40s meant that the pond almost always froze hard enough to allow skating and sliding. During one long spell of hard frost the ice reached a thickness of seven inches and took so long to thaw in the continuing cold that it lasted well into spring and reputedly had to be broken up using chains to allow the early yachting competitions to commence. In another year the ice reached the weight-bearing stage, then a partial thaw melted it round the edges, but a subsequent period of hard frost cured the problem. During a day of warm weather when the ice was crowded, the thinner stuff round the edges quite suddenly became too thin, trapping hundreds in the middle of the pond. The antics of those marooned attracted passers-by until there was a large crowd of spectators egging and cheering on those who were forced to pluck up the courage and make a dash for it over the thin stuff! Many didn't make it without a soaking, and by that time the main body of ice was weakening also.

The Linthouse/Whiteinch vehicular ferry, 1928. At this period crossing the river other than by the Finnieston tunnel or the bridges upstream towards the city centre required a ferry journey, with services at six pedestrian and three vehicular crossing points operated by the Clyde Navigation Trust (CNT) between Linthouse and KGV Bridge. Crossings provided by the CNT were free, but the two other services downstream, provided by Renfrewshire and Dunbartonshire County Councils, were fare-paying. The vehicle ferries docked in specially constructed basins which accommodated about two thirds of their length so that they were kept clear of other river traffic. The original vessels of the design shown here were steam-powered, with elevating platforms to allow for tidal height variations of between ten and fourteen feet. A more modern version (both types had twin smoke stacks) was introduced in 1938 with diesel–electric propulsion and somewhat lighter construction. The platform was wide enough for three lanes of road vehicles, and when the gates were thrown open on the arrival of a busy crossing, there was a kind of Wild West stampede among carters (horse-cart drivers) to be first at the top of Holmfauld Road. Like other main roads then this was cobbled, so the din created by the steel-shod wheels of the racing carts must have been around the maximum level permissible by the decibel scale introduced in later years. The 'hut' at top centre of the superstructure was the captain's 'cabin', from which he had a commanding view for docking manoeuvres and looking out for approaching river traffic. By the late 1930s wheeled traffic was half horse-drawn and half motorised, but even then these vessels were still called the horse ferries. The early ferries carried vehicles only, but the newer ones had accommodation on one side of, and separate from, the vehicle deck for a limited number of passengers who could sit on life rafts which doubled as seats. Access to this space was by a kind of drawbridge that was pivoted up before departure so that the foot-treads became a protective barrier.

A second view of the Linthouse / Whiteinch vehicular ferry. Passenger services were provided by smaller vessels such as the one just visible on the right of the picture on the facing page. One hazardous aspect of using the ferry was the steps which had to be negotiated when boarding and leaving. Although lying at a fairly shallow angle, a stumble at the top of them could mean rolling down into the water. There were two long-handled boat hooks within easy reach, one on each side of the dock wall, and although I never saw these used I heard stories of people – usually drunk – having to be rescued and sent on their way dripping. The access at the head of the stairs was of necessity quite narrow, restricting the passage to single individuals to avoid crowds causing accidents at busy times. This was somewhere for the ordinary individual and not just the elderly to avoid at workers' finishing time! In the descent the stairs widened out, as seen here on the right, to aid docking in wild weather. When strong winds and spring tides both pushed in the same direction the boats could be carried well away from their usual path and crossing times could be doubled or trebled. Apart from the stairs hazard, there was the difficulty of actually getting on and off the boat. The ferries were bidirectional with their prows ending in a rounded, open point, allowing them to come into contact with the stairs. In calm conditions this meant a simple step on or off, but in rough weather, although held by a stout rope looped round one of the bollards in the corner of each step by the ferryman, the ferry could surge around quite violently.

'Chums, 1937'. This is one of the many photographs taken by *Daily Record* photographers to boost circulation of the paper. Photographers were sent to residential areas of the city to gather up groups of children whose picture would be taken for inclusion in a subsequent issue. This one was taken in the back court at 6 Clachan Drive. Today, press photographers are a relatively familiar sight and in a similar situation would cause only mild interest, but at that time it was a rare occurrence to see a professional photographer and therefore much more exciting. My mother happened to be working at the kitchen sink in our top flat at 12 Skipness Drive when she saw from the window the group being gathered. She ran a comb through my hair and sent me round with the admonition 'hurry up or you'll be too late'. The only names recalled are Alister Wishart, second from the left, middle row, and Jimmy Nicol on the chair in the front row. I'm the shortest one in the back row.

Renfrew Road at Hardgate Road, *c*.1950. Stephen's battery-powered locomotive is returning empty waggons and a van from the yard to Shieldhall goods station. The track junction is curving out of frame to the right past the end of Hardgate Road and into the goods yard seen in the picture on page 35. The original Shieldhall sewage works stood on the left behind the brick wall; in the 1960s it was enlarged to cover much of the northern end of Hardgate Road and the by then disused goods yard. In the distance is the tenement block in Govan Road at the foot of Moss Road where a German parachute landmine struck on 13 March 1941, killing 69 people. A petrol station occupies the site of the three closes destroyed, and this must be one of the last examples of an identifiable bomb site left in the city. Nearer the camera are the trees in the grounds of the Southern General Hospital. Just this side of the hospital boundary, which was also Glasgow City boundary, there was a leafy lane which ran up to Shieldhall farm, worked at that time by Christie Clelland. This was a favourite walk of my grandfather's and mine, taken to study and identify the greenery and wildlife found there, mostly birds. Beyond the farm was Coila Park recreation ground, set up by Alexander Stephen's for its workers. Beyond that again on the other side of a footpath (a continuation of Langlands Drive) was the field where the art deco Luma Lamp Factory, also seen in the picture on page 35, was built. Behind the adverts on the right was the Clyde Sawmill & Wood Storage Co. Its distinctive sheds had Belfast type roofs and walls with vents to keep the contents dry. The board seen above the locomotive cab carried the woodyard company's name.

Alexander Stephen began shipbuilding more than 250 years ago in Burghead, and over the following 100 years the company he founded expanded and moved to other towns around the north-east coast of Scotland. In 1850 a yard was set up on the Clyde, initially at Kelvinhaugh, but the company had to move from there to allow excavation of Queen's Dock to begin in the 1870s, establishing its shipyard on the Linthouse Estate in 1870. Richardson's map of 1796 indicates that at that time the estate belonged to Sprent Shortridge. Linthouse Mansion, illustrated here, survived the setting up of the shipyard to be used as the yard offices until expansion over the decades saw the main office block built in Holmfauld Road in 1915. From the late 1930s up to 1945 I was constantly interested in what was going on on the river, and used to spend time at an ideal vantage point on the stretch of riverbank upstream from the ferry terminals. When walking past Stephen's main gate in Holmfauld Road just north of the office block, I was struck by the appearance of an old building a little way inside near the slips, and in later years wondered if it could have been the mansion. A number of photographs consulted in recent years seem to confirm that it was.

The Scottish Co-operative Wholesale Society's (SCWS) factories, Shieldhall, *c*.1960. The first co-op to be set up in Britain, even before Rochdale, was the Govan Co-operative Victualling Society which lasted from the mid-1700s to 1905. (Rochdale can claim to be the oldest because of holding written proof which the Govan society lacked.) The Kinning Park Co-operative Society was set up in the 1860s, and after consultation with other co-ops agreement was reached to set up a wholesale buying and manufacturing organisation. From this the SCWS was born. A large area of ground was purchased at Shieldhall and factories were built to make many of the more popular items then available. At its peak more than 5,000 people worked there. When the tram route was extended to Renfrew a twin track siding was laid in Bogmoor Road (lower right) to ease the congestion caused by the number of vehicles required to transport the SCWS employees.

Key:

1. Footwear factory
2. Pickle factory
3. Confectionery factory
4. Tobacco factory
5. Catering department
6. Artisan and juvenile clothing factory
7. Preserve factory
8. Engineering department
9. Architectural (works) department
10. Printing department
11. Transport department
12. Wines and spirits section
13. Coffee essence factory
14. Tea department
15. Sheet metal factory
16. Chemical sundries department
17. Funeral undertakers monumental yard
18. Furniture factory
19. Bedding factory
20. British Luma Co-operative Electric Lamp Society Ltd.
21. Medical block

This is the gents' department of the Shieldhall tailoring factory, probably No. 6 in the aerial view, where three-piece suits were made up. At this time my mother and her sister Molly worked here. Molly, a vest (waistcoat) machinist, has been circled, while my mother, a trouser machinist, is somewhere among the unidentifiable faces in the background. The co-op had a reputation for being a good employer that paid higher wages than other companies, and competition for jobs was fierce among potential workers. My maternal grandmother was a staunch supporter of the co-operative movement, buying everything from their shops, and I used to wonder whether this patronage had anything to do with her daughters' luck in landing jobs there. The most sought-after jobs were in the tobacco and confectionery factories.

Shieldhall dining rooms, *c.*1890. In the 1930s part of the field on the left of the picture on page 35, unbuilt on at this time and lying between Bogmoor Road and Renfrew Road after it made a ninety degree turn round the newly constructed KGV Dock, was used to store barrels containing pickles for the bottling plant. One day, along with a group of pals on an exploring / scavenging expedition, we discovered that on reaching through the boundary railings the bungs of the nearest barrels were accessible and could be removed. This gave us access to the onions, cauliflower and other pickles!

Now part of the Southern General Hospital, Merryflatts Poorhouse (seen here in 1928) opened as Govan Combination Poorhouse in 1872. To the south, near Langlands Drive, there was a separate building designated as an asylum, while another detached building to the north was the actual hospital. The original main entrance to the Southern General in Govan Road was through a narrow stone arch suitable for the horse-drawn vehicles of early times, but enlargement of the medical facilities from the 1960s rendered it impractical and a new, much wider entrance was opened to the west after which the old one was sealed off. During my family history researches I came across the legend 'died at 1301 Govan Road' many times! For years I wondered why this was so, until one time I was driving into the old hospital entrance and noticed the number 1301 on it. Moss Road was reconstructed in the 1920s to a standard which made it one of the widest in the area. Then in the 1960s it was further widened to become part of the Clyde Tunnel approach road, and to make space for the new road the boundary railings seen here were moved back about 60 feet. In the clock tower, behind the slats below the clock, there is a large bell which hasn't been used for many years.

From the early 1900s the buildings of Shieldhall Combination Hospital for infectious diseases were known simply as the fever hospital. There were eight wards in total, plus the superintendent's house and service buildings, all of which were laid out within a square plot of land off the south side of Langlands Drive. The drive was an unmade cul-de-sac outwith Merryflatts' boundary railings that continued on as a footpath to Hardgate Road near Coila Park. Anyone suffering from an infectious disease such as scarlet fever or smallpox was brought here in a special dark green vehicle known as the fever van. When it arrived in the street to make a call it caused a feeling of dread. Similar events typically attracted a group of curious children, but when it was the fever van everyone kept clear, watching from a distance with apprehension. As a member of a squad of urchins who sometimes ventured in this direction, we always walked on the other side of the road when passing along Langlands Drive to keep as far away from the place as possible. The geriatric unit of the Southern General now occupies this site.

Of a plain design but with a steep mansard roof, the David Elder Infirmary (seen here in 1925) was demolished in the 1990s. It was founded for charity cases and injured workmen and stood on ground at the north-east corner of the Moss Road / Shieldhall Road junction. The main entrance was by a short drive off Moss Road. The seldom-used avenue in the foreground was entered through a double-leaf gate flanked by pedestrian entrances set well back on the pavement in the cutaway corner at the road junction. In the 1930s this layout was imprinted in my memory in a rather violent way. Where the avenue crossed the pavement to join the road, barriers had been erected as a form of pedestrian control. As a young boy, when out on a Sunday afternoon stroll with my grandfather, I was able to walk erect under the barriers. Some time elapsed before we passed this way again, and when I tried to walk under in the usual way I got a severe crack on the head which left me momentarily dazed. After commiserating, granda had family members laughing at the way I was learning about growing up when we arrived home!

The Elder Cottage Hospital in Drumoyne Drive. The relief carving above the doorway of a mother nursing a baby indicates that it was intended to be a maternity home, but it became a general hospital operating in tandem with Merryflatts and specialised in geriatrics. A nurses' home was built here on the right, and all the buildings including the hospital have been preserved by conversion to flats. Langlands Road, visible in the foreground, looks unmade. On the 1858 Ordnance Survey map Langlands farm is situated on the right, just behind where the hospital was built.

Langlands Road with the junction of Cara Drive on the left, *c.*1920s. Much of the land leading down to the river here was owned by the Stephen family of shipbuilding fame, and when some of it was developed for housing five of the streets in the area were given names of the family's children. Cara Drive was formerly Agnes Drive, Mambeg Drive was Margaret Drive, and St Kenneth Drive was Katherine Drive. Kennedar Drive was Stephen Drive and Skipness Drive was George Drive. Drive Road (originally Royal Terrace) branches off at the end of the terrace in this picture (built 1898), with the trees of Elder Park lying beyond it. In the distance is the chimney of a cabinet factory in Crossloan Road. The entrance seen in the pavement on the left was the start of the long track to Mid Drumoyne farm, while nearby to the west there is another much shorter lane which once led to West Drumoyne farm, a strip of which was sold off to become Pirrie Park, the sports ground for workers at Harland & Wolff. In the 1930s this lane continued on past the farm and over a rise to Shieldhall Road at Mallaig Road. The land west of this path as far as the David Elder Infirmary was a field in which cattle grazed up to the 1950s. Farms were often referred to by the name of the occupant, and as far as memory can be trusted West Drumoyne was Miller's farm. Reliable informants tell me that Shieldhall farm was worked during this period first by Danny Fairservice who lived in a tenement in Burghead Drive, followed by Christie Clelland who also lived in Govan. Hamilton's was a name applied to Hardgate farm opposite the main entrance to the SCWS complex in Renfrew Road.

Katherine Drive (now St Kenneth Drive) is in the foreground of this 1928 view of Elderpark Primary School, with Stephen (Kennedar) Drive leading off to the left. The tenement in the left background, and St Kenneth's Church on the right (now demolished) are in Hutton Drive. The long chimneyhead in a gable above the church belongs to the single tenement close in Katherine Drive off Royal Terrace (Drive Road). Royal Terrace was unique in having the dwellings numbered continuously (both even and odd) on one side only because it was assumed that there would be no building allowed on Elder Park opposite at any time in the future (and indeed no buildings have been erected there to this day). During the Second World War the district air raid siren was mounted on the roof of the school.

My grandmother Mary Chambers was an activist in the rent strike of 1915. During the First World War extra workers were required in industry, particularly shipbuilding, leading to a great influx of people to Govan and a strain on housing. Through their factors, unscrupulous property owners attempted to impose rent increases, not just on the new arrivals but on existing tenants as well. The strike campaign, which came to a head in September, was supposed to take place on a nationwide basis but was almost exclusively confined to Glasgow and Clydebank. Much of the protest action was centred in Govan. The most serious aspect of the situation was that it affected wives and parents of soldiers then fighting on the battlefields of France. Local women used this point to great effect by getting the forces authorities, through the men themselves, to complain that while they were fighting and dying for their country their wives and families were being harassed and penalised by greedy landlords. Of the large number of tenants who refused to pay the rent increases, the property owners selected a few and took them to court. When tenants lost their cases and still refused to pay, warrant sales of their possessions were authorised, and sheriff's officers were instructed to enforce them. Committees were formed by groups, mainly of women, who set up an early warning system to alert residents to the approach of the sheriff's officers. A large crowd would assemble round the close where the house was situated ready to obstruct the officers. Police were then summoned, but still the crowd defied them and refused to disperse, and at that point the officer in charge usually backed off. Along with several others, Mary Chambers and her brother Charles Himsley, who lived in the same close, were summoned for non-payment of the rent increases. Mary got off but Charles was fined, the fine being paid by a collection. These two photographs show No. 13 Hutton Drive (very close to where the photograph opposite showing the demonstration was taken), and a group including my grandmother, who is second from the left. Other members of the group are, left to right, my mother, Agnes; grandfather, Joe Chambers; and my mother's sister, Molly. The photograph was taken at the rear of Shieldhill Fever Hospital.

When this photograph came to light it proved to be of intense interest. It shows a scene being enacted in front of the close at 10 Hutton Drive quite in keeping with what would be expected to cause the police, long before the days of tear gas, riot shields and batons, to retire without doing anything. Of particular interest to me is the lady who has been circled, who bears a striking resemblance to my grandmother, Mary Chambers.

Image courtesy of The Herald & Evening Times (Newsquest) Ltd.

An early twentieth century view of Govan High School in Langlands Road. One day in the mid-1930s when I was out walking with my granda we were confronted by an amazing sight at this location. Coming slowly along the road, almost filling it from side to side and moving west towards us, was a multi-wheeled trailer carrying a large boat being hauled by a traction-engine. Shepherded by men on foot to check for clearances, it was being moved from McLean's boatbuilding yard in Uist Street. Taking his pipe from his mouth and pointing with its stem, granda said 'That lifeboat's going to John Brown's in Clydebank [where he worked] to be put on the *Queen Mary*'. I must have been about three or four years old at the time, but that sight has remained with me over the decades. Each time I saw the ship, in photographs or anchored in the firth during the war, I used to look at the lifeboats and wonder which one it was I saw 'sailing' along Langlands Road. When recalling the event in later years I wondered why it was being moved west, then realised that it was going either to Shieldhall Dock to be lifted into the water, or to the ferry slip at Renfrew to be slipped in there for onward transport to Brown's.

This photograph of the fire which destroyed Govan High School in the 1970s was taken by the late Sidney Smith, former member of the Govan Reminiscence Group, who lived within sight of the school in one of the terraced houses at the top of Drive Road.

C K Fletcher
Drawn CIRCA 1934

SAINT CONSTANTINE'S SCHOOL
FROM NIMMO DRIVE 1992

Due to the absence of photographs of St Constantine's School in the period shortly after it opened in 1928, I've included Chris Fletcher's excellent drawing of the building with its open verandas. At the time of the first air-raid on Glasgow on 19 July 1940 I was in a class on the top floor. The weather was clear and sunny, and we were in the course of normal classroom activity when the sound of a plane was heard. Immediately there was a noise – the first but not the last time I was to hear it – which became apparent was the sudden whistle of bombs falling followed by loud explosions which shook the building. A picture of the event in my mind is of our teacher leaning off his high chair at a steep angle, the more quickly to get on his feet, and dashing to the door with a look of alarm very evident on his face, and yelling 'come on children, everybody out as quick as you can'. We were rushed out and along the veranda with the other classes in a rapidly growing stream, urged on by panic-stricken teachers, to the north wing of the building and into the cloakroom there. As we were crammed into the barely adequate space, I felt more afraid of being crushed there than the danger of whatever it was we were fleeing from. Teachers would have been following directives laid down by the authorities in assembling us in these three small rooms in each wing of the building, although what would have happened if a bomb had struck one of them at that moment does not bear thinking about. There was much coming and going of staff as they tried to find out what had happened and what was expected of them, and after a time we were released with instructions to go straight home and report to our mothers without fail.

This class photograph was taken at St Constantine's School in 1938. The following are the only names recalled:
1, Robert Watson; 2, James Lawson; 3, T. McLeod; 4, Sergio Innocenti (son of the owners of the Linthouse Cafe); 5, J. McMenamin; 6, J. Farrell; 8, H. Murphy; 9, P. O'Brien; 10, E. McLauchlin; 11, ___ Mulligan; 13, Gerry Belton; 14, Michael McAuley; 15, Francis Sharp; 16, George Rountree; 18, Alec Shades; 19, Pat Sloan; 21, Jean Denny?; 24, Theresa McKenna; 25, J. Campbell; 26, James Fox; 27, ___ Campbell; 29, ___ Stewart; 36, Jean Flannigan. I showed this to the St Constantine's head teacher in the early 1990s. She studied it for a while, then said '42 pupils, how on earth did they manage'!